A New Resonance

10

Emerging Voices in
English-Language Haiku

Edited by Jim Kacian & Dee Evetts

A New Resonance 10:
  Emerging Voices in English-Language Haiku

© 2017 by Jim Kacian
for Red Moon Press
All Rights Reserved

First Printing

Published by
Red Moon Press
PO Box 2461
Winchester VA
22604-1661 USA
www.redmoonpress.com

ISBN 978-1-947271-00-5

All work published with permission of the individual authors or their accredited agents.

Cover Painting: Wolf Kahn, *Blue Sky, Grey Trees* (2011)
Oil on canvas.
Addison Ripley Gallery, Washington DC.
Used with permission.

Foreword

It is to our considerable surprise and delight that we are celebrating, with this volume, the culmination of our second decade of engagement with the future bright stars of English-language haiku. What began as a one-off at the end of the previous century now realizes its tenth iteration. The mission for the New Resonance series has evolved over this time, from a showcase for rising talent into something considerably more. We now see New Resonance as a place where a poet of any pedigree and prior success might successfully exhibit a substantial amount of work in a single venue, still a remarkably rare event in the haiku world. And while we still maintain that this is one step toward recognition on a larger scale, and hence the adjective "emerging" still obtains, we also recognize that an even more palpable effect of this recognition is the creation of a highly specific community, the New Resonance community, the members of which will nearly all go on to publish their own books and have a larger forum for their work and ideas. But they will have started here, and that will be a fact that will gather them together in their own minds and in ours. This community has had and will continue to have a collective effect on the growth and development of English-language haiku. It has been our pleasure to have been a part of this process, and one we hope to continue well into the future.

Jim Kacian & Dee Evetts
Series Editors

A New Resonance

10

S. M. Abeles

Mary Frederick Ahearn

Johan Bergstad

Meik Blöttenberger

Mark E. Brager

Sondra Byrnes

Bill Deegan

Chase Gagnon

Elmedin Kadric

Marcus Liljedahl

Joe McKeon

Stella Pierides

Rob Scott

David Serjeant

Shloka Shankar

Els van Leeuwen

Dick Whyte

S. M. Abeles

Attorney

Born 20 June 1971
West Orange, New Jersey
Currently resides
Washington, D.C.

The poet reports provisional positions in the midst of his life's unfolding. We comprehend this through quiet statements and observations based upon a considerable degree of self-knowledge. This awareness seems to be the source of the writer's ability to meet life's circumstances creatively. There is a strong sense of the vertical in Abeles' haiku, of deep roots and personal history ("old neighborhood"). This permeates the relationship poems as much as those that draw upon solitary experiences. Along with glimpses of migration and return ("first star"), there is a sense that these memories have been knitted into a present curiosity about where things will lead, and how they may be influenced.

Credits

deep summer	*Modern Haiku* 44.3
her hand	*Modern Haiku* 46.2
fireflies	*Under the Basho* 2015
I count	*Failed Haiku* 1
petal by petal	*Frogpond* 38.2
reawakening	*Modern Haiku* 46.2
the first bite	*Shamrock* 27
city limits	previously unpublished
no matter	*Frogpond* 37.2
a grown man	*World Haiku Review* January 2014
dusk	*Under the Basho* 2015
first star	*Presence* 52
all the magic	*Under The Basho* 2013
old neighborhood	*The Heron's Nest* 15.3
deeper cuts	*Under The Basho* 2013

"the first bite" was Runner-Up for Best Senryu in *Shamrock*'s Reader's Choice Awards 2014; "old neighborhood" also appeared in *Beyond the Grave: Contemporary Afterlife Haiku* (Middle Island Press, 2015).

deep summer . . .
the give of the porch
beneath bare feet

her hand
in my pocket
driftwood

fireflies the pipe we pass between us

I count
all her freckles
starry night

petal by petal the yellow rose on her inner thigh

reawakening inside her rib cage murmur of autumn

the first bite
is all I want
wild pear

city limits
the wind whispers
what I want it to

no matter how I try to dilute you absinthe

a grown man
on a swing . . .
nightfall

dusk I glide into my comic book ending

first star
and then another—
the long way home

all the magic
you attribute to me . . .
snowflakes

old neighborhood
I inhale
my ghost

deeper cuts
in the cutting board
the ways I've changed

S. M. Abeles

Mary Frederick Ahearn

Johan Bergstad

Meik Blöttenberger

Mark E. Brager

Sondra Byrnes

Bill Deegan

Chase Gagnon

Elmedin Kadric

Marcus Liljedahl

Joe McKeon

Stella Pierides

Rob Scott

David Serjeant

Shloka Shankar

Els van Leeuwen

Dick Whyte

Mary Frederick Ahearn

Retired Caseworker

Born 6 February 1947
Williamsport, Pennsylvania
Currently resides
South Coventry, Pennsylvania

From this group of haiku the one that might stand out as emblematic of the poet's experience, and outlook on life, is "second thoughts". This poem vividly conveys a sleeve being plucked, a physical manifestation of indecision and reappraisal, of having to step back physically but also mentally or emotionally. Elsewhere this theme can be observed to play out in various guises. Acts of devotion are leavened—subverted even—by hints of license ("a flash of Pan"). Sobriety interweaves with playfulness ("spice aisle"), alternatives present themselves ("wild geese"). Alongside runs an occasionally visible thread of nostalgia ("winter trees"). Past felicities are revisited, yet without any sense of longing or regret, but rather as reference points or navigational aids.

Credits

poems I used to know	*Frogpond* 35.3
winter trees	previously unpublished
wild geese	*Sharing the Sun*
scent of summer hay	previously unpublished
willows green	*Modern Haiku* 44.1
swimming	*Frogpond* 36.1
waiting for the rain	previously unpublished
rain follows rain	*A Hundred Gourds* 3.2
the last of the rain	*Acorn* 30
second thoughts	*Frogpond* 34.3
muffled voices	*Frogpond* 37.2
a flash of Pan	*Frogpond* 38.3
days you believe	*Issa's Untidy Hut* April 16, 2014
spice aisle	*A Hundred Gourds* 3.1
walking the wrack line	*Acorn* 29

Sharing the Sun"- HSA Members Anthology 2010

"willows green" first appeared in the haibun "One Hundred Pages"; "swimming" first appeared in the haibun "Another Name"; "a flash of Pan" also appeared in *Every Chicken, Cow, Fish and Frog: Animal Rights Haiku* (Middle Island Press, 2016), and received The Haiku Foundation's Touchstone Award for Individual Poems (2015).

poems I used to know
a rabbit slips
under the hedge

winter trees
as darkness falls
once I wore black lace

wild geese
coming or going
New Year's Day

scent of summer hay
across the snowfields
barn lights

willows green
where the river bends
spring again

swimming
alone in the ocean
my dream of flying

waiting for the rain
the right way
to tell you

rain follows rain
in muted voice
the congregation's response

the last of the rain
your apology
lingers

second thoughts—
rose thorns
catch my sleeve

muffled voices
from the confessional
shadows on the wall

a flash of Pan
in the goat's eye
barn shadows

days you believe
days you can't
a trick of the light

spice aisle
a wink
from a stranger

walking the wrack line
at low tide—
poems I know by heart

S. M. Abeles

Mary Frederick Ahearn

Johan Bergstad

Meik Blöttenberger

Mark E. Brager

Sondra Byrnes

Bill Deegan

Chase Gagnon

Elmedin Kadric

Marcus Liljedahl

Joe McKeon

Stella Pierides

Rob Scott

David Serjeant

Shloka Shankar

Els van Leeuwen

Dick Whyte

Johan Bergstad

Psychologist / Writer

Born 5 March 1973
Gävle, Sweden
Currently resides
Hedemora, Sweden

The proportion of haiku poets who are psychologists suggests a special kinship between the disciplines. Perhaps it's a sensitivity to emotional nuance, to be found both in human behavior as well as natural imagery, that pairs them. This results, in Bergstad's case, in a kind of restraint, an understatement that is not currently fashionable. For instance, rising to greet the dawn with the birds is a natural joy, but "leav[ing] the birds/un-named" evokes a special kind of sympathy. There are other appreciations of what is perhaps better left unsaid, whether found in the weight of words, the taking of a hand, of simply the joy of a son's sharing the good news of spring's return.

Credits

spring sun	*Acorn* 21
rumble of thunder	*Snowdrops*
before and after	*Frogpond* 31.3
deeper into the woods	previously unpublished
midnight sun	previously unpublished
light of dawn	previously unpublished
a still life	*Frogpond* 30.3
memorial grove	*Snowdrops*
sparrows	*Silently the Morning Breaks*
peace	previously unpublished
timber train	*The Heron's Nest* 10.3
winter evening	*Blåeld* 2
airport	previously unpublished
drifting ice	*Silently the Morning Breaks*
music	*Silently the Morning Breaks*

"spring sun" and "memorial grove" were selected to appear in "Haiku of Sweden" (The Haiku Foundation, 2016); "timber train" also appeared in *Nest Feathers: Selected Haiku from the First 15 Years of The Heron's Nest* (The Heron's Nest, 2015), and in *Kamesan's World Haiku Anthology on War, Violence and Human Rights Violation* (CreateSpace, 2013). *Snowdrops: Eleven Swedish Haiku Poets* (Bokverket, 2009); *Silently the Morning Breaks: Ten Swedish Haiku Poets* (Östasieninstitutet, 2008).

spring sun
my boy tells everyone
the same secret

rumble of thunder
a cat jumps down
onto the piano

before and after the bell its ring

deeper into the woods
his voice
deeper

midnight sun
my new friend wants us
to share secrets

light of dawn
we leave the birds
un-named

a still life
and, just outside the frame,
an old guard

memorial grove
snowflakes disappear
into snow

sparrows
on both sides
of the military fence

peace or new porsche

timber train
a thought about
Auschwitz

winter evening
my wife thinks we argue
in the wrong way

airport
the weight of
your words

drifting ice
by the bridge
I take your hand

music
on the upper floor
I write again

S. M. Abeles

Mary Frederick Ahearn

Johan Bergstad

Meik Blöttenberger

Mark E. Brager

Sondra Byrnes

Bill Deegan

Chase Gagnon

Elmedin Kadric

Marcus Liljedahl

Joe McKeon

Stella Pierides

Rob Scott

David Serjeant

Shloka Shankar

Els van Leeuwen

Dick Whyte

Meik Blöttenberger

Non-Profit Coordinator

Born 28 February 1962
Baltimore, Maryland
Currently resides
Hanover, Pennsylvania

Many of these poems feel singularly self-contained. That is, each could conceivably represent the sketch or framework for a short story, with a different and quite distinct protagonist appearing in each poem. This is not to say there is no cohesiveness here. The reference to "all the lives I've lived" affirms that the various personae we glimpse are but aspects or incarnations within a single life. Blöttenberger seems inclined to embrace that diversity. As to the days ahead, he foresees "no revisions." And not inconsistent with this stance is an apparent empathy with other species (hens, a gorilla, a dead sparrow).

Credits

dog days *A Hundred Gourds* 4.2
deadheading daisies *Presence* 51
paper wasp nests *Frogpond* 37.1
speaking in previously unpublished
just hens *A Hundred Gourds* 5.1
painting the house *Frogpond* 38.3
grey-tinged sky *Presence* 51
birdsong before dawn Kaji Aso Contest 2015
stone bridge Ito En Contest 2015
sea cave *The Heron's Nest* 17.1
wolf moon *Acorn* 36
winter zoo *The Heron's Nest* 17.1
fresh snow *Hedgerow* 49
fading light A Little Haiku Contest 2016
sunrise *Frogpond* 36.1

"paper wasp nests" also appeared in *big data: The Red Moon Anthology of English-Language Haiku 2015* (Red Moon Press, 2016); "birdsong before dawn" took Third Prize in the Kaji Aso Haiku Contest 2015; "stone bridge" was a semifinalist in the Ito En Haiku Contest 2015; "fading light" won Honorable Mention in the Little Haiku Contest 2016.

dog days settling in slippers of sand

deadheading daisies
still no desire
to remarry

paper wasp nests—
emails from my siblings
unanswered

speaking in
my second tongue
a lily's long throat

just hens in the rain without a verb

painting the house numbers Pluto a planet again

grey-tinged sky
searching for arrowheads
in a furrowed field

birdsong before dawn
all the lives
I've lived

stone bridge
meeting me halfway
the cold wind

sea cave
the thoughts I keep
inviting back

wolf moon
not letting anger
get the rest of me

winter zoo
a gorilla turns
its back to the crowd

fresh snow covering the dead sparrow in me

fading light
the mountain
more fragile

sunrise
no revisions
expected

S. M. Abeles

Mary Frederick Ahearn

Johan Bergstad

Meik Blöttenberger

Mark E. Brager

Sondra Byrnes

Bill Deegan

Chase Gagnon

Elmedin Kadric

Marcus Liljedahl

Joe McKeon

Stella Pierides

Rob Scott

David Serjeant

Shloka Shankar

Els van Leeuwen

Dick Whyte

Mark E. Brager

Communications Specialist

Born 18 April 1963
Detroit, Michigan
Currently resides
Columbia, Maryland

The quotidian has long been the stuff of haiku, but what makes it of interest is our response to it. Brager's poems evince a life like many others, with its joys and pains, its health and sickness — and the realization that these things are inextricably bound together. A son "floating away/from me" can occasion the thrill of a loved one gaining a new skill while realizing the inevitable separation that is taking place every moment. Our own mortality can cause us to chase our own limits (the memorable "threshold dose") or come to terms with our shortcomings ("the pressure inside/the confessional"). Perhaps, with persistence and a bit of luck, our world, too, "falls/into place."

Credits

swimming lesson	*haijinx* 4.1
pond's edge	*Acorn* 35
one face	*DailyHaiku* Cycle 12
dust motes	*Frogpond* 37.1
speaking in tongues	*Frogpond* 37.2
circling crows	*bones* 7
daybreak	*Modern Haiku* 43.3
no handlebars	*Under the Basho* 2014
deep breath	*Prune Juice* 9
thunderhead	*Moongarlic* 2
etched in pollen	*The Heron's Nest* 17.4
sunset	*The Heron's Nest* 17.2
long winter's night	*Under the Basho* 2013
kaleidoscope	*Acorn* 30
driftwood	*Under the Basho* 2014

"one face" also appeared in *faces and places anthology 2015*; "thunderhead" also appeared in *big data: The Red Moon Anthology of English-Language Haiku* 2014 (Red Moon Press, 2015), and *Dwarf Stars* (Science Fiction Poetry Association, 2015); "etched in pollen" also appeared in *galaxy of dust: The Red Moon Anthology of English-Language Haiku* (Red Moon Press, 2016).

swimming lesson
my son floating away
from me

pond's edge
my reflection
casting stones

one face
then the other . . .
falling leaf

dust motes the silence after the eulogy

speaking in tongues autumn leaves

circling crows the weight of the subjunctive

daybreak
turning on
the reality show

no handlebars coasting the threshold dose

deep breath—
the pressure inside
the confessional

thunderhead losing myself in big data

etched in pollen the smallest word of God

sunset . . .
debating Rothko's
use of red

long winter's night sorting the nails from the screws

kaleidoscope . . .
the sky falls
into place

driftwood the pull of your amniotic sea

S. M. Abeles

Mary Frederick Ahearn

Johan Bergstad

Meik Blöttenberger

Mark E. Brager

Sondra Byrnes

Bill Deegan

Chase Gagnon

Elmedin Kadric

Marcus Liljedahl

Joe McKeon

Stella Pierides

Rob Scott

David Serjeant

Shloka Shankar

Els van Leeuwen

Dick Whyte

Sondra J. Byrnes

Retired

Born 29 December 1944
Great Bend, Kansas
Currently resides
Santa Fe, New Mexico

We like to think we are gliding smoothly through life, one moment transitioning to another, but in fact we are caught again and again by an endless series of tiny hooks of reality that snag us and slow our momentum. Byrnes is especially keen in noticing these moments of dwell, both in the physical world (the halt of a zipper; wool in barbed wire; even the limbo between worlds) and in our verbal representations of it (what is said, or not said, or nearly said; and the structure of language itself). Her particular gift is to suggest how the real and the literal interact—a physical kick may escalate into a linguistic tumble, chaos in the wake of a storm summons a verbal analog—and to grant them, and us, the time it takes for realization.

Credits

saturday night	previously unpublished
in the garden	previously unpublished
crescent moon	previously unpublished
assumptions	previously unpublished
he kicks	*Moongarlic* 1
wool snagged	previously unpublished
yesterday	previously unpublished3
a housefly	previously unpublished
summertime	*tinywords* 15.2
harvest moon	previously unpublished
thanksgiving leftovers	*tinywords* 15.1
winter-lit	European Kukai 2013
facing a knot	previously unpublished
storm blackout	previously unpublished
tea	*The Heron's Nest* 17.4

A version of "winter-lit" received Second Place in the European Kukai 2013.

saturday night searching for a verb

in the garden
after last night's storm
a dangling modifier

crescent moon
i meant what i
didn't say

assumptions
caught in the teeth
of a zipper

he kicks a stone into an argument

wool snagged
on a pasture fence
my maiden name

yesterday
i sat here too
dry stream bed

a housefly drags the heat from place to place

summertime
let the screen door
bang

harvest moon
even if that was all
there was

thanksgiving leftovers
all the things we
didn't say

winter-lit
the blue tint
of silence

facing a knot
in the wooden pillar
zazen

storm blackout
the bardo between now
and whatever

tea
all the time
it takes

S. M. Abeles

Mary Frederick Ahearn

Johan Bergstad

Meik Blöttenberger

Mark E. Brager

Sondra Byrnes

Bill Deegan

Chase Gagnon

Elmedin Kadric

Marcus Liljedahl

Joe McKeon

Stella Pierides

Rob Scott

David Serjeant

Shloka Shankar

Els van Leeuwen

Dick Whyte

Bill Deegan

Financial Professional

1954
Brooklyn, New York
Currently resides
Mahwah, New Jersey

The psychological factors in human behavior are of particular interest to this poet. This much is openly declared in his phrase "all we think we desire", while elsewhere it appears more allusively, in such poems as "making cold camp" and "Father's Day". This perceptiveness with regard to motives and undercurrents is well served by a close observation of detail, as exemplified by the small movement of a foot glimpsed in a voting booth, telegraphing something. Many of these signals are sourced in the poet's feeling for ordinariness filled with interest. Allied with this is an emotional range that can encompass the gentle irony of "all those years in accounting" as well as the plain hilarity of a near-clean getaway from some family event, foiled at the last.

Credits

casting for bonefish	previously unpublished
a second one	*The Heron's Nest* 17.3
all those years	previously unpublished
hiking	*Frogpond* 38.3
making cold camp	previously unpublished
Father's Day	*Frogpond* 37.2
beneath the curtain	*Modern Haiku* 45.3
bits of scandal	*Frogpond* 38.1
the smile	previously unpublished
balance of power	previously unpublished
turning the paper	*tinywords* 15.1
egg white	*Frogpond* 35.3
escaping the relatives	previously unpublished
what's hidden	previously unpublished
last night's snow	*Evening Stillness*

"a second one" received Special Mention in *The Heron's Nest* 2015 Readers' Choice Awards; "egg white" was short-listed for The Haiku Foundation's 2012 Touchstone Award for Individual Poems. *Evening Stillness: Haiku Circle 10th Year Anthology* (Haiku Circle, 2016).

casting for bonefish
all we think
we desire

a second one last look   cherry blossoms

all those years in accounting
never the same river twice
they say

hiking without a phone the subtext of maple

making cold camp
a bonfire
across the lake

Father's Day—
blueberry pie softens
the conversation

beneath the curtain
a foot on its heel
election day

bits of scandal
heard in passing—
hot coffee grounds

the smile of the
iron doorstop cat . . .
autumn rain

balance of power
tipping into twilight
the cliff swallow

turning the paper
to first light
lone commuter

egg white
slipping through my fingers
winter sunrise

escaping the relatives
the car door
frozen shut

what's hidden
and what's not—
day moon

last night's snow
slips from a branch—
first of January

S. M. Abeles

Mary Frederick Ahearn

Johan Bergstad

Meik Blöttenberger

Mark E. Brager

Sondra Byrnes

Bill Deegan

Chase Gagnon

Elmedin Kadric

Marcus Liljedahl

Joe McKeon

Stella Pierides

Rob Scott

David Serjeant

Shloka Shankar

Els van Leeuwen

Dick Whyte

Chase Gagnon

Writer / Photographer

Born 17 February 1995
Detroit, Michigan
Currently resides
Detroit, Michigan

Few whose childhoods have been spent coping with the recent urban American reality of poverty and abandonment have ventured into the rarified atmosphere of haiku, with its codes of appropriateness and occasionally fey ethos. Fewer still have had the resource to write while still in the grips of that reality—age and circumstance mitigate against it. But Gagnon has had the wherewithal to use language as a coping mechanism, and the results are so raw and immediate as to make us feel as though we have all lived through an existence of drugs, violence, loneliness and despair. Geography may be fate, but aspiration remains individual, and one poet's hopes may be found here in these powerful short glimpses of what there is to overcome.

Credits

busted knuckles	*Prune Juice* 17
who I used to be	*Prune Juice* 16
old neighborhood	*No Regrets*
city of the damned	*Prune Juice* 15
greyhound station	*No Regrets*
lonely night	*A Hundred Gourds* 4.2
last of my money	*Lakeview International Journal* 4.2
buffering	*No Regrets*
darkening sunset	*The Sound of Shadows*
self-inflicted scars	*No Regrets*
lonely night	*moongarlic* 5
almost better	*No Regrets*
abandoned train station	*Prune Juice* 18
morning moon	*cattails* 2
no regrets	*Haiku Scout* 3

No Regrets (2015) and *The Sound of Shadows* (2014) are self-published chapbooks.

busted knuckles . . .
my father's blood mixing
with mine

who I used to be . . .
the empty streets
of the motor city

old neighborhood . . .
volunteers painting
over my graffiti

city of the damned
a homeless man
god-blesses me

greyhound station . . .
the junkie's
far-away eyes

lonely night
the high from a stranger's
vicodin

last of my money
the palm reader says
I'm rich in many ways

buffering—
the girl in this porno
with the same name as my ex

darkening sunset
I watch a mosquito fill
with my blood

self-inflicted scars
I pray for forgiveness
from myself

lonely night
I slide my lips
across the harmonica

almost better
to be alone . . .
summer stars

abandoned train station
the peace of waiting
for nothing

morning moon—
a stranger's scent
in my bed

no regrets—
fresh graffiti
on the dilapidated boxcar

S. M. Abeles

Mary Frederick Ahearn

Johan Bergstad

Meik Blöttenberger

Mark E. Brager

Sondra Byrnes

Bill Deegan

Chase Gagnon

Elmedin Kadric

Marcus Liljedahl

Joe McKeon

Stella Pierides

Rob Scott

David Serjeant

Shloka Shankar

Els van Leeuwen

Dick Whyte

Elmedin Kadric

Administration

Birthdate 20 July 1990
Novi Pazar, Serbia
Currently resides
Helsingborg, Sweden

Sometimes inertia can feel like inevitability. Kadric seems especially sensitized to the pre-ordained, and his terrifying monoku based on a children's game—"rock paper scissors war"—can feel like doom. Inertia means that what is in motion tends to remain in motion, and so tumbleweed becomes an emblem of always moving on to the next place, and love can be construed to already reside in the DNA of a daisy. But what's at rest also tends to remain at rest, and so a daydream can last into the night, and small talk runs along the surface of the *fait accompli*. Personal interjections then—be they the willed manifestation of persimmons, or the unadorned and prosaic act of kicking a stone—are where we take on what is, and begin turning it to what will be.

Credits

i start	*Failed Haiku* 4
roadside diner	*Modern Haiku* 46.3
rock	*A Hundred Gourds* 4.4
inspired by	*Acorn* 36
making	*tinywords* 14.1
dry leaves	*tinywords* 15.2
how it's plucked	*Frogpond* 38.1
because	*Otata* July 2016
after	*hedgerow* 67
her origami bird	*The Heron's Nest* 17.1
autumn nightfall	*A Hundred Gourds* 5:1
making small talk	*Modern Haiku* 45.2
where we used	*Under the Basho* 2015
driving home	*Prune Juice* 14
just like that	*Failed Haiku* 3

"roadside diner" also appeared in *galaxy of dust: The Red Moon Anthology* 2015; "driving home" also appeared in *big data: The Red Moon Anthology* 2014.

i start
the day
dreaming

roadside diner
the soldier buys himself
some time

rock paper scissors war

inspired by
a true story
tumbleweed

making
a long story short
fall

dry leaves—
helping my father
with his death poem

how it's plucked out of the daisy love

because she said so persimmons

after the wedding ring cold white halo

her origami bird
I learn
by unfolding

autumn nightfall teaching her first-born subtraction

making small talk . . .
the gravel path
to the graveyard

where we used to use wildflowers

driving home—
nobody to hold
the ashes

just like that
I start kicking
another pebble

S. M. Abeles

Mary Frederick Ahearn

Johan Bergstad

Meik Blöttenberger

Mark E. Brager

Sondra Byrnes

Bill Deegan

Chase Gagnon

Elmedin Kadric

Marcus Liljedahl

Joe McKeon

Stella Pierides

Rob Scott

David Serjeant

Shloka Shankar

Els van Leeuwen

Dick Whyte

Marcus Liljedahl

Opera Singer

Born 30 March 1972
Malmö, Sweden
Currently resides
Göteborg, Sweden

One characterization of Europe is that it is ancient and weary, worn-out, and to read some of these poems by an artist employed in the re-creation of its high art, it might seem as though this were true — the trees are old, there are bones in the rain, and the gods have been disfigured. But that is not the whole of what is here: there is also hope. This hope resides primarily in looking for signs, in the natural world ("the language of birds"), in the human ("the chapel's stained glass"), and most of all, from within (a morning that is "dreamless" is worthy of note). What is of significance is that "our shadows reach / beyond the ruins", and that the city is indeed "eternal." Perhaps, if we can find the signs, we will be able to find the way back to the time when the sky was "endless", and all was new.

Credits

distant thunder	*Frameless Sky* 4
beyond barbed wire	*A Hundred Gourds* 5.2
war zone	*Frogpond* 38.2
cherry blossoms	previously unpublished
hospital sky	previously unpublished
wave after wave	previously unpublished
between	*otoliths* 34
snake skin	*A Hundred Gourds* 3.4
inside	*Bones Journal* 4
dreamless morning	previously unpublished
first frost night	previously unpublished
eternal city	previously unpublished
winter sun	previously unpublished
dusk	previously unpublished
childhood streets	previously unpublished

"distant thunder" and "beyond barbed wire" both first appeared as parts of tan renga.

distant thunder
the memories of my father
all worn out

beyond barbed wire
a sky pierced
by endless swallows

war zone an ancient god's disfigured face

cherry blossoms
some white bones
in the still rain

hospital sky
the sun moving slowly
behind old trees

wave after wave
the unspeakable constantly
on our tongues

between distance and closeness the language of birds

snake skin
the path to you
unfolds behind me

inside a seagull's cry my other life

dreamless morning
still no sign
of flowers falling

first frost night
deep in your voice
that other woman

eternal city
a fountain goddess
collects coins

winter sun
our shadows reach
beyond the ruins

dusk
in the chapel's stained glass
I find your face

childhood street
the sky just as endless
as I remember it

S. M. Abeles

Mary Frederick Ahearn

Johan Bergstad

Meik Blöttenberger

Mark E. Brager

Sondra Byrnes

Bill Deegan

Chase Gagnon

Elmedin Kadric

Marcus Liljedahl

Joe McKeon

Stella Pierides

Rob Scott

David Serjeant

Shloka Shankar

Els van Leeuwen

Dick Whyte

Joe McKeon

Human Being

Born 10 September 1948
Chicago, Illinois
Currently resides
Strongsville, Ohio

There is a strong sense of autobiography in McKeon's work, yet simultaneously a degree of removal or detachment. These are the poems of an experienced adult, but his range includes memories from throughout the various stages of his life. It is as if the poet had stepped back from the canvas in order to gain a better view of it. We note a proclivity for the precise and telling image, such as the slicing cake knife or the glow of a cigarette. These create not mere vignettes, but serve to anchor the memories or experiences firmly in very particular instants. Some of these moments (for example "weekly skype" and "new headstone") convey intimations of the poet's own mortality. And yet recollecting the blueness of the globe, or noticing the charms of a different voice, help to recover the innocence experience may tend to dull.

Credits

retirement party	*Failed Haiku* 1.3
church steps	*HSA Members Anthology* 2016
snow crocus	*Harold G. Henderson Contest*
the Christmas	*Harold G. Henderson Contest*
empty nest	previously unpublished
shooting star	*Frogpond* 39.3
weekly skype	*A Hundred Gourds* 5.4
arrangements made	*Frogpond* 39:1
flag-draped casket	*cattails* April 2014
pollen count	*Modern Haiku* 45.3
new heaadstone	previously unpublished
blind date	*Modern Haiku* 47.1
lost	previously unpublished
peek-a-boo moon	previously unpublished
first day of school	*Modern Haiku* 47.3

"snow crocus" won Honorable Mention in the Harold G. Henderson Haiku Contest in 2015; "the Christmas" won 3rd Place in the Harold G. Henderson Haiku Contest in 2014.

retirement party
the cake knife slices
through my name

church steps
an old man leaning
on the wind

snow crocus
my grandson asks
if I have dreams

the Christmas
after we told them
artificial tree

empty nest
snowfall deepens
the silence

shooting star
the distance between wants
and needs

weekly skype
my father and I compare
mole hills

arrangements made . . .
the glow of dad's cigarette
in a dark room

flag-draped casket
three volleys fill the air
with sparrows

pollen count
no one suspects
the truth

new headstone
all that matters
in a dash

blind date
the way she says
tomato

lost in the wild part of me found

peek-a-boo moon
she answers my question
with a question

first day of school
most of the globe
is blue

S. M. Abeles

Mary Frederick Ahearn

Johan Bergstad

Meik Blöttenberger

Mark E. Brager

Sondra Byrnes

Bill Deegan

Chase Gagnon

Elmedin Kadric

Marcus Liljedahl

Joe McKeon

Stella Pierides

Rob Scott

David Serjeant

Shloka Shankar

Els van Leeuwen

Dick Whyte

Stella Pierides

Poet / Writer

Born 21 August 1952
Athens, Greece
Currently resides
Neusaess, Germany / London

The nature of the real has changed in our time, and how to register this change is Pierides' chosen task. She brings to it full cognizance of her historical antecedents—she alludes to Greek philosophy ("Plato's cave") and mythology (slyly, in "atlas"), Japanese poetry ("a frog jumps in"), and even French existentialism ("*mala fide*"). But where she comes down, for all her far-flung excursions of the mind, is immediately before her: a wave, the tides, the mountains, and especially the precariousness of ice. At the same time, it is her challenge to make these things real at the far end of a blinking cursor on a backlit screen, all the while remaining aware that what she leaves behind "in the cloud" may be no more than just those few blinking sensations.

Credits

atlas	*A Hundred Gourds 5.3*
rumours	*Blue Print Review 30*
it happens	previously unpublished
unfurling fronds	*Beyond The Grave*
Plato's cave	*Bones 2*
pending	*Bones 2*
another country	*Frogpond 36.2*
a frog jumps in	*Sonic Boom 4*
sleepless night	*Bones 9*
mice-nibbled sack	*"The Year of Light"*
washing	*"The Year of Light"*
river tides	*Tinywords* 28 December 2015
walking on ice	*A Hundred Gourds 4.2*
mountains	previously unpublished
mala fide	*Frogpond 38.3*

"another country" first appeared in the haibun "Parcels", was reprinted in *Feeding the Doves: 31 Short and Very Short Stories, and Haibun* (Fruit Dove Press, 2013) and included in "Haiku Journey," a video entry to HaikuLife 2015 (The Haiku Foundation Haiku Film Festival); "a frog jumps in" first appeared in the haibun "Intertextuality", and was reprinted in "Recipe" in *Of This World: 48 Haibun* (Red Moon Press, 2017); "sleepless night" was reprinted in *Full of Moonlight* (Haiku Society of America, 2016); "*mala fide*" was included in "Arrivals," a video entry to HaikuLife 2016, (The Haiku Foundation Haiku Film Festival). *Beyond The Grave: Contemporary Afterlife Haiku* (Middle Island Press, 2015). "The Year of Light," EarthRise Rolling Haiku Collaboration 2016 (The Haiku Foundation).

atlas
the weight
of my dreams

rumours—
rush of water
over stone

it happens to the best of us ocean wave

unfurling fronds
my digital legacy
in the cloud

Plato's cave each day a new shadow

pending your answer the moon's glare

another country
the snowflakes taste
of salt

a frog jumps in—
intertextuality
for beginners

sleepless night formatting loneliness

mice-nibbled sack . . .
edging closer to
the real

washing my hands of spring rain

river tides where have I been

walking on ice . . .
my full attention
to the moment

mountains know what I mean

mala fide—
taking another look
at the moon

S. M. Abeles

Mary Frederick Ahearn

Johan Bergstad

Meik Blöttenberger

Mark E. Brager

Sondra Byrnes

Bill Deegan

Chase Gagnon

Elmedin Kadric

Marcus Liljedahl

Joe McKeon

Stella Pierides

Rob Scott

David Serjeant

Shloka Shankar

Els van Leeuwen

Dick Whyte

Rob Scott

Teacher

Born 17 July 1967
Melbourne, Australia
Currently resides
Stockholm, Sweden

Scott here provides numerous variations on the theme of one thing overlaying or covering up another. These depictions are eloquent of currents flowing below the surface of events—as in treats being clandestinely slipped to a pet, or a muttered remark overheard. Alternatively the revelation of layers takes the form of a subtle transformation or shift, as found in "after the lullaby" or "wind gust". Through it all we get a strong sense of the poet's ability to cope with whatever comes his way. There is a bonus as well in his sports-related poems, where we are given indelible examples of feelings made visible: the taunting batsmanship of a cricketer, the magnetic sway of spectators at a soccer match.

Credits

arguing about politics	*Frogpond* 29.2
after the lullaby	*Frogpond* 24.2
day moon	*failed haiku* 1.5
last ball	previously unpublished
injury time	previously unpublished
dying sun	*Frogpond* 31.3
wind gust	*failed haiku* 1.4
naked trees	previously unpublished
third day of rain	*Presence* 2002
thick fog	previously unpublished
beginning	previously unpublished
day off	previously unpublished
Monday morning	*paper wasp* 15.2
winter solstice	previously unpublished
waking from a dream	*failed haiku* 1.5

"arguing about politics" also appeared in *big sky: The Red Moon Anthology of English-Language Haiku 2006* (Red Moon Press, 2007); "third day of rain" was commended for the *Haiku Presence* Award 2002; "Monday morning" also appeared in *where the wind turns: The Red Moon Anthology of English-Language Haiku 2009* (Red Moon Press, 2010).

arguing about politics—
dad feeds the dog
under the table

after the lullaby—
her slow breathing
a lullaby

day moon—
her first
white lie

last ball before lunch
the batsman lets it go
with a flourish

injury time—
the corner kick bends
with the crowd

dying sun
a sacrifice fly
holds the light

wind gust—
out of nowhere
we start an argument

naked trees
I hear what she says
under her breath

third day of rain
her stance
softens

thick fog—
a whole day
in my head

beginning
to get used to the snow
it melts

Monday morning
a sigh exits
the lift

day off—
I listen to the bus
until it's gone

winter solstice—
an old friend
remembers me first

waking from a dream—
I lose my dad
again

S. M. Abeles

Mary Frederick Ahearn

Johan Bergstad

Meik Blöttenberger

Mark E. Brager

Sondra Byrnes

Bill Deegan

Chase Gagnon

Elmedin Kadric

Marcus Liljedahl

Joe McKeon

Stella Pierides

Rob Scott

David Serjeant

Shloka Shankar

Els van Leeuwen

Dick Whyte

David Serjeant

Local Government Officer

Born 25 October 1971
Manchester, England
Currently resides
Chesterfield, England

In the following poems we find an evocation, and equally a celebration, of everyday life in the UK. The routines of school and the workplace are observed and embraced, albeit with a distinct vein of irony and humor. Along the way we receive glimpses of a more contemplative persona ("spring breeze", "lost in thought"). Occasionally, there are darker or more ominous details: the reminder of a fire truck's essential purpose, the resentment carried by someone in a tedious job. But the tone is prevailingly light, and finds its epitome when, following an art gallery visit, the poet takes a dig at what passes for sophistication.

Credits

spring breeze	*Presence* 40
two nil down	*Blithe Spirit* 25.2
school fair	*Simply Haiku* 6.4
dance class melée	*Presence* 35
minimalist	*Blithe Spirit* 21.1
barking	*Blithe Spirit* 20.1
a patchwork	*A Hundred Gourds* 3.2
after the downpour	*Notes from the Gean* 3.2
talk of redundancies	*Smithereens*
my colleague	*Riverbed* 3
telling her 'no'	*Lakeview International Journal* 1.2
still talking	*Shamrock* 11
lost in thought	*Shamrock* 16
a late spring	*Blithe Spirit* 20.2
in the centre	*Shamrock* 16

"after the downpour" also appeared in *A Splash of Water: The Haiku Society of America Members' Anthology 2015*. Smithereens (*https://issuu.com/daveserjeant/docs/smithereens*, 2013).

spring breeze—
somewhere in the valley
playtime

two nil down—
gleefully my daughter
tallies the swearwords

school fair—
a trace of smoke
on the fire engine

dance class melée
my weekly nod
to the other dad

minimalist
the
gallery
loo

barking at his dog the leash snaps taut

a patchwork of tarmac the road to the tip

after the downpour
the evening sky
all over the road

talk of redundancies
spring bulbs emerge
in corporate colours

my colleague
flirting with the workman
endless summer rain

telling her 'no'
her shoulders listen
to the reasons

still talking
after I've gone
the widow next door

lost in thought
a breeze I can't feel
glows the embers

a late spring
the blackbird tries
a different song

in the centre
of the merry-go-round
the fair worker's scowl

S. M. Abeles

Mary Frederick Ahearn

Johan Bergstad

Meik Blöttenberger

Mark E. Brager

Sondra Byrnes

Bill Deegan

Chase Gagnon

Elmedin Kadric

Marcus Liljedahl

Joe McKeon

Stella Pierides

Rob Scott

David Serjeant

Shloka Shankar

Els van Leeuwen

Dick Whyte

Shloka Shankar

Freelance Writer

Born: 23 May 1989
Mumbai, India
Currently resides
Bangalore, India

One of the bespoke traditions of haiku has been its focus on the emotional impact of images, foregoing an intellectual rigor for a felt truth. While this remains largely intact, there has been a broadening in our appreciation of what actually succeeds in the brief compass of such poems. One such direction has been the confessional, and it is in this vein that Shankar excels. Her clipped diction ("meaning what you mean", "inside the womb", among others), eclectic interweaving of personal and "natural" fact ("wormhole", "white space", and ditto), and intruiguing re-interpretations of idiom ("square one", *in medias res*", "cat's cradle") results in a telegraphic style that is idiosyncratic and instantly recognizable.

Credits

ad infinitum	*Quatrain.fish* February 2016
wormhole	*Under the Basho* 2016
Oxford comma	*Failed Haiku* 1.4
meaning	*Failed Haiku* 1.4
eraser	53rd Caribbean Kigo Kukai 2014
split pomegranate	*Prune Juice* 17
in medias res	*the other bunny* June 2, 2015
before and after	*The Zen Space* July 2015
doodling	*one link chain* February 2016
inside the womb	previously unpublished
the lag	*Frozen Butterfly* 2
gossamer	*A Hundred Gourds* 5.1
odd sock	*Frozen Butterfly* 2
tipping the balance	*shufPoetry* 5
right where	*A Hundred Gourds* 4.2

"eraser" won First Place in the 53rd Caribbean Kigo Kukai, August 2014, and appeared in *naad anunaad: an anthology of contemporary world haiku* (Pune, India: Vishwakarma Publications, 2014) as did "before and after".

ad infinitum i go back to square one

wormhole the time it takes to remember

Oxford comma—
the attention
you pay me

meaning what you mean spring rain

eraser
my mother's mistakes
no longer mine

split pomegranate
I fall a little more in love
with myself

in medias res the dreamscape of our lives

before and after the wasteland white butterflies

doodling a memory the size of my fist

inside the womb the prototype of art

the lag between breaths white space

gossamer the length of a dream

odd sock
wondering what I saw
in you

tipping the balance a nightjar's call

right where we started cat's cradle

S. M. Abeles

Mary Frederick Ahearn

Johan Bergstad

Meik Blöttenberger

Mark E. Brager

Sondra Byrnes

Bill Deegan

Chase Gagnon

Elmedin Kadric

Marcus Liljedahl

Joe McKeon

Stella Pierides

Rob Scott

David Serjeant

Shloka Shankar

Els van Leeuwen

Dick Whyte

Els van Leeuwen

Early Childhood Educator

Born 16 March 1976
Sydney, Australia
Currently resides
Sydney, Australia

To be assailed by doubts and hesitation is not necessarily to feel lost. The poet's voice here tends rather toward cautiousness, notably in the search for appropriate words and in the weighing of meanings. Much is inexplicit, and the reader is left to ponder significances, in the perhaps obsessive picking at a label, or the leap of a fairground horse. Not everything is spelled out for us, and the work is stronger for it. The enigmatic details ring true even while they defy explication. And if the weight of contingencies might have become oppressive, we are also given the unalloyed and infectious optimism of a paper boy whistling in the rain.

Credits

moving day	previously unpublished
dew	previously unpublished
spring breeze	*Modern Haiku* 45.1
cloud drift	previously unpublished
after rain	previously unpublished
nightfall	previously unpublished
whatever he meant	*A Hundred Gourds* 3:.3
middle age	*Frogpond* 37.3
proposal	previously unpublished
I have the word	previously unpublished
turning from him	previously unpublished
untangling	previously unpublished
how to say it	previously unpublished
distant flock of birds	*A Hundred Gourds* 3.1
through endless rain	*The Heron's Nest* 10.4

moving day
a doll's house
on the street

dew
in the astro turf
her sad smile

spring breeze
an urge to pull weeds
from a stranger's grave

cloud drift
I ask my father
for directions

after rain
the minister's comfortable room
for doubts

nightfall
picking at the price tag
on the bible

whatever he meant
lingers
            gardenia

middle age
the leap
of a carousel horse

proposal
how my footfall changes
on the bridge

I have the word
he can't find
the wind stills

turning from him
to the stars
a log shifts in the fire

untangling
Christmas lights
a storm rolls in

how to say it
the grip I use to pick up
broken glass

distant flock of birds
the neighbour's phone
rings on

through endless rain
the whistle
of the paper boy

S. M. Abeles

Mary Frederick Ahearn

Johan Bergstad

Meik Blöttenberger

Mark E. Brager

Sondra Byrnes

Bill Deegan

Chase Gagnon

Elmedin Kadric

Marcus Liljedahl

Joe McKeon

Stella Pierides

Rob Scott

David Serjeant

Shloka Shankar

Els van Leeuwen

Dick Whyte

Dick Whyte

University Lecturer

Born 13 September 1978
Aotearoa
Currently resides
Te Whanganui-a-Tara, Aotearoa

The best haiku poets have been able to invoke the political without becoming politicized — who can forget the image of the *daimyo* bent before a blossom? Similarly they have been able to evoke their present circumstances. These are precisely the realms wherein Whyte dwells. He shows his broad sympathies commiserating with his fellow men and women ("no jobs", "poverty") as well as with other creatures ("blowfly!", "winter sky"); he has a keen sense of where history has occurred, and its consequences in real terms ("where soldiers slept"); he finds the human concern in the natural ("summer heat") — all of which place him firmly in the camp of Issa. And while even the Japanese master despaired at the end, Whyte is capable yet of sustaining hope ("spring") in the most traditional of haiku fashions.

Credits

no jobs	previously unpublished
between	previously unpublished
poverty	*Daily Haiku* Cycle 8, 2009
possibility	previously unpublished
minimum wage	*Haiku News* June, 2012
dawn	*Mainichi* Haiku Contest 2012
summer heat	previously unpublished
blowfly	previously unpublished
infinite sky	previously unpublished
stone by stone	previously unpublished
scattered clouds	previously unpublished
winter sky	*c.2.2. Anthology of Short Verse*
where soldiers	*Ambrosia* 3
dusk	previously unpublished
spring	previously unpublished

"minimum wage" and "winter sky" also appeared in *A Book Of Sparrows* (Four Shades Press, 2016); "dawn" won Honorable Mention in the *Mainichi* Haiku Contest 2012; *c.2.2. Anthology of Short Verse* is published by Yet To Be Named Free Press, 2013.

no jobs
in the paper again . . .
first snow

between
the richest and poorest . . .
shadows lengthen

poverty—
no matter where you go
the moon

possibility: more more more
                        stars

minimum wage i envy the sparrow

dawn—
the white of a lily
not yet white

summer heat this too is political

blowfly!
being your friend
isn't easy

infinite sky the comfort of hyperbole

stone by stone the pull of the river

scattered clouds the only answer i get

winter sky . . .
the sparrow doesn't know
i'm black

where soldiers
once slept and died—
a spider's home

dusk—
the blackbird sings
even louder

spring,
i'll be better
then